1924: Ella Jenkins is born in St. Louis, Missouri. Her mother moves the family to Chicago when Ella is very young.

1939: World War II begins in Europe.

1941: Japanese fighters bomb Pearl Harbor in Hawaii, and the United States enters the war.

1942: Ella graduates from DuSable High School.

1942–48: Ella has various jobs, including packing war rations at the Wrigley chewing gum factory. Each little box of rations contains hardtack (a hard, saltless cracker), a small can of Spam, a tiny pack of cigarettes, a pack of Doublemint gum, and a chocolate bar.

During this time, Ella also works at the University of Chicago, delivering classified mail to scientists working in secret to develop the atomic bomb.

1945: American fighters drop atomic bombs on Hiroshima and Nagasaki, Japan. The two cities are devastated, and World War II ends.

1948: Ella leaves Chicago for California. She lives with friends in Berkeley before moving to San Francisco.

1949: Ella becomes codirector of the Codornices Village community center and playground in Albany, California. She is paid 75 cents an hour.

1951: Ella graduates from San Francisco State College (now University) and returns to Chicago.

For Ella, who made the music, and Bernadelle, who understood.
And for my mother, who made sure I listened. —T. N. T.

To Danny. —E. D.

Library of Congress Cataloging-in-Publication Data available.

ISBN 978-1-4521-7064-0

Manufactured in China.

Art direction by Amelia Mack and Jennifer Tolo Pierce.
Design by Jennifer Tolo Pierce.
Typeset in Chiswick Sans and Gabriela.
The illustrations in this book were rendered digitally in Procreate.

10 9 8 7 6 5 4 3 2 1

Chronicle Books LLC
680 Second Street
San Francisco, California 94107

Make a Pretty Sound

A Story of Ella Jenkins—
The First Lady of Children's Music

By **Traci N. Todd** *Illustrated by* **Eleanor Davis**

chronicle books · san francisco

Amid the blare and bleat
of taxicabs,
the screech of high-up trains,
the tamborines that ring
as preachers preach
and choirs sing—
amid the pool hall–gritty
beat of the city

a little girl named Ella whistles with the birds.

Little girls shouldn't whistle,

her mother says.

But Ella wants to make a pretty sound.

Ella is a South Side girl,
a Bronzeville bird,
skipping in streets that
smell of sweets and
black-eyed peas.

Everywhere she looks
there are
brown-skinned people,
bronze-skinned people,
just like her.

Outside this part
of Chicago,
outside that
Bronzeville line,

the White City is not kind
to bronze-skinned girls.
The White City would rather
they stay in their place—

but little birds
will learn to fly.

Ella rises
on the rhythm of spelling words;
snap, clap, Mary Mack
recess rhymes;
songs Señorita Rojas sings
in Spanish class at school.

Ella's favorite spot is a record shop
where she hears music from Morocco, India,
and all around the world.

The rhythms are exciting,
the languages are beautiful,
and every voice
is an invitation.

At night
Ella's mother mops and hums,
her brother jabs at air,
Big Bill Broonzy plays from Aunt Willie Mae's jukebox,
and Uncle Flood puts on his music vest.

From a pocket—which will it be?—
he pulls a silver slip,
brings it to his mouth and—
how Ella loves that sound!

The way the notes wheeze and wail,
the way her uncle rolls and sways
until Ella can hear, almost see, Louisiana,
where Uncle Flood learned to play the blues.

When he has an extra dime or two
Uncle Flood takes Ella to dazzling Bronzeville
music halls where
Sassy sings,
Basie jumps,
and Louis Armstrong blows his horn.

But the coolest cat is Cab Calloway.
With his peacock strut he calls to the crowd
and they respond:

back and forth,
back and forth,

like the beating
of wings.

Ella rises
on the rhythm of picket lines
under picket signs
outside stores with pretty things
Black folks aren't allowed to touch,
outside restaurants where
Black folks aren't allowed to eat.

Sometimes she goes inside,
takes a seat,
and ***waits***

and ***waits***

and ***waits***

in silence.

Ella is tired of waiting.
She leaves Chicago behind
on a train heading west.

Ta-rum, ta-rum it hums,
carrying her farther from home
than she has ever been.

When the train heaves a final sigh,
Ella is in a city of water,
of bridges and fish,
of foghorns yawning on the bay.

Ella makes her way north
to a village quickly built
for the rush of workers—
Black and white—
who forged the ships that fought a war.

When the war ended, the workers stayed.
They raised their children—
Black and white—side by side.
Together.

The children are the heart
of the village—
the harmony and song—
skipping rope, throwing jacks,
and playing table tennis.
Together.

And did you know?
Ella is a table tennis champion!

Back home, when boys said,

"Girls can't play!"

this girl
showed them
how it's done.

She shows the children how
tap bounce tap
to listen to the rhythm,
tap bounce tap
find the rhyme,
tap bounce tap
flick their wrists
tap bounce tap
right on time!

And just like that, Ella becomes a teacher.

Ella is a student, too.
On days she isn't with the children,
she chases brilliant ideas under the covers
and around the pages of thick college books—

left, right, down, up,

piecing together brilliant ideas
of her own.

And at night . . .

Congas ***pop!***
Claves ***click!***
Maracas ***shick-shick-shick!***
West African, Cuban, Dominican beats
catch Ella's ears
(her heart, her breath),
shout to her feet, her hips, her arms,

She meets Armando Peraza,
the great conguero
who tumbles from ***rumble!*** to ***smack!***,
from ***pop!*** to ***paaaah!***
with the spread of his fingers
and the shape of his hands.

He shows Ella how, again and again.
Ella watches, listens,
and learns to play in her own Ella way.

And she can hardly wait to show the children.

When she returns to the village,
she pushes the tennis tables aside,
makes room for oatmeal boxes, plastic pails, and tin cans—
anything to make a pretty sound.

She tells the children to watch. To listen.
To ***clap***, ***smack***, ***pop***, and ***paaah!***,

each in their own way.

OATS

Over their music
in a voice sweet and clear,
Ella sings
songs the children know,
songs she makes up on the spot,
songs her mother hummed
while her brother jabbed at air.
Songs about growing up in Bronzeville,
about whistling with the birds.

And all at once,
all at once,
Ella knows:

It is time to go home.

These are not the streets Ella
skipped through as a girl.
(She is different, too.)

The city has a bolder sound—a

feet on the ground, signs in the air,
fists raised knocking on the
door of freedom

kind of rhythm.

we shall overcome,
we shall not be moved,
we have had enough
kind of beat.
FREEDO NOW
EQUAL RIGHTS NOW
EQUAL RIGHTS NOW

Ella keeps time on her drum,
lifts her voice, and sings,

Oh freedom,
oh freedom,
oh freedom
over me.

She sings before a sea of thousands.
She sings before a King.

But Ella's song is for the children,
for the hope she feels when she
hears their voices,
for all that music can teach them
about themselves

and about each other.

She visits them at summer camps and schools,
brings them drums to play, rattles to shake, bells to ring.

Sometimes, from her pocket, she pulls a silver slip—

and plays ***Uncle Flood's blues***.

Ella fills records with the children's voices.
They sing of love and welcome
while Ella plays tambourine.

Sometimes she sings, too—
a call to every child.

A hope that even if they
don't understand all her words,

they'll understand this:

You sing a song,

and I'll sing a song,

Children write to Ella
from far away, begging her to come.
Once again she leaves
Chicago behind and travels farther
than she has ever been.

JAMBO
ELLA JENKIN

¡Bienvenida Srta. EllaJe
11

She returns from every trip overflowing
with new melodies, harmonies, stories to tell;
greetings to share;
suitcases bursting with instruments to shake and click and strum.

And she can hardly wait—

to show
the children.

And the children can hardly wait—
hardly wait!—to see her.

Sing me a song
again, do . . .

Together, they will ***make a pretty sound***.

About Ella Jenkins

To many, Ella Jenkins is known as the First Lady of Children's Music. At a time when music for children was mostly silly songs and movie soundtracks, Ella knew that music could be a powerful tool to teach basic information and cultural awareness. She believed that every sound, rhythm, language, and dialect should be celebrated, especially if it made a child feel seen and heard. And she has influenced every children's musician who has come after her.

Ella was born in St. Louis, Missouri, on August 6, 1924. Her family moved to Chicago, Illinois, where she grew up on the South Side, in a neighborhood called Bronzeville. Bronzeville was home to many Black families who left the racial oppression of southern cities hoping for better, safer lives in the North. But northern cities—like Chicago and New York—often weren't very welcoming, and Black folks were forced to live in specific neighborhoods. As the number of Black families grew and Black neighborhoods weren't allowed to expand, housing became overcrowded and unsafe. Still, neighborhoods like Bronzeville in Chicago and Harlem in New York were thriving centers of Black culture.

Ella and her brother, Tom, were raised by their mother, Annabelle; their uncle Flood (his real name was Floyd Johnson); and their aunt Willie Mae. Ella's mother worked as a maid, and Uncle Flood worked at the steel mills in Gary, Indiana. Like most families in Bronzeville, Ella's moved every year, hoping to make it to a nicer area each time. No matter where they moved, they were always close enough to see music at the Regal Theater on 47th Street, where Ella saw Cab Calloway for the first time.

When he performed, Calloway used a technique called call-and-response, which has roots in West Africa and can be found in jazz, blues, and church music. Cab would call—or sing a phrase—and the audience would respond by repeating the phrase. This call-and-response pattern would later define the way Ella sang with children.

After Ella graduated from high school, she had trouble finding work because of the limited options for Black women. A friend suggested she move to San Francisco for better opportunities.

Like Chicago, San Francisco and the Bay Area were attractive places for Black people to settle after leaving the South, especially during World War II, when ship building became a big industry. Southern white people also came to the Bay Area looking for work during the war. To accommodate the new workers, Bay Area cities quickly built housing complexes like Codornices Village. When the village was first built, Black people were assigned less desirable housing, but in 1946, the village managers moved families around so that housing was distributed fairly. The managers also made sure that the village had an even number of Black families and white families. (This balancing act happened at the *expense* of Black families, whose numbers, and therefore needs for housing, were greater.) Codornices Village was one of the few places in the United States where Black people and white people lived side by side and where their children played and went to school together. After growing up in racially segregated Chicago, this was an incredible thing for Ella to see. In 1949, she became codirector of the Codornices Village community center and playground, and she began experimenting with making music for and with children.

Living in San Francisco influenced Ella in other ways, as well. She lived in a dormitory for Jewish women (although she wasn't Jewish, she was welcomed, but had to live in the basement), and her housemates taught her Jewish traditions and songs. She also went to nightclubs where she once sipped soda with Billie Holiday. She was exposed to a musical mix from West Africa, Cuba, and the Dominican Republic. She was especially enchanted by the music of master percussionists Armando Peraza (who later played with Carlos Santana) and Chano Pozo (a friend and mentor to trumpet great Dizzy Gillespie), as well as incomparable singer Miguelito Valdés.

After graduating from San Francisco State College (now University) in 1951 with a degree in sociology and minors in recreation and child psychology, Ella returned to Chicago. She was hired as a program director for teens at the YWCA and in 1956 was invited to appear on a local television show called *Totem Club*. The next year, she released her first record, *Call-and-Response Rhythmic Group Singing*. Later she was a regular visitor on *Mister Rogers' Neighborhood*.

In the 1960s, Dr. Martin Luther King Jr. came to Chicago to highlight the racist practices that prevented Black people from being able to afford good, safe housing. In June of 1964, he held a rally at Soldier Field, Chicago's huge outdoor football stadium. Many musicians performed before a crowd of thousands, including Ella. She had always been active in civil rights, ever since her brother took her with him to protests when she was a young girl.

Ella's career has spanned nearly 70 years and touched generations of children and their grown-ups. In the earliest days of her career, she introduced young children of many ethnicities to the beauty and power of Black music and of music from all over the world. In 2004, the Recording Academy recognized her accomplishments with a Grammy Lifetime Achievement Award, and in 2005, the album *cELLAbration: A Tribute to Ella Jenkins* won a Grammy for Best Musical Album for Children. In 2023, she turned 99 years old—what a life she has lived!

Author's Note

Early in this book, I refer to Chicago as the "White City." This was an actual nickname for Chicago that originated in 1893, when Chicago hosted the World's Columbian Exposition. The exposition was a monthslong fair that included carnival rides—like the first-ever Ferris wheel—food innovations, and visions of the future. (However, Black people were not allowed to exhibit at the exposition, making any vision of the future incomplete.) Many of the Columbian Exposition's buildings were made of a gleaming white material that was so impressive, people referred to it as the White City. The name later came to stand for Chicago itself, especially as local activists fought against systemic racism.

Acknowledgments

Thank you to Steve Malk, who first asked me to write about Ella and whose children's love for her music reminds me of my own. Thank you to Ella Jenkins and Bernadelle Richter, who always made time for me. And finally, I must thank Tim Ferrin, who, in the course of making *Ella Jenkins: We'll Sing a Song Together*, a documentary film about Ella, was unfailingly generous with resources and support.

Selected Bibliography

Jenkins, Ella. *Call-and-Response Rhythmic Group Singing*. Recorded in 1957. Smithsonian Folkways Recordings, 1998, compact disc. Liner notes.

———. Interviews with the author. October 2016.

———. Oral history interview with Larry Crowe. August 5, 2002. The HistoryMakers Digital Archive, A2002.133, session 1, tape 2, story 1. http://thmdigital.thehistorymakers.com/iCoreClient.html#/&i=9025.

———. Oral history interview with Larry Crowe. August 5, 2002. The HistoryMakers Digital Archive, A2002.133, session 1, tape 4, story 3. http://thmdigital.thehistorymakers.com/iCoreClient.html#/&i=9044.

Jenkins, Ella, with Arnold Radel and children from the Cross-Cultural Family Center of San Francisco. *Travellin' with Ella Jenkins: A Bi-lingual Journey*. Recorded in 1979. Smithsonian Folkways Recordings, 1989, compact disc. Liner notes.

Jenkins, Ella, with children from the LaSalle Language Academy of Chicago. *Sharing Cultures with Ella Jenkins*. Smithsonian Folkways Recordings, 2003, compact disc. Liner notes.

Jenkins, Ella, with the Chicago Children's Choir. *Hopping Around from Place to Place!* Vol. 1. Educational Activities, 1983, 33⅓ rpm, and 1999, compact disc. Liner notes.

———. *Hopping Around from Place to Place!* Vol. 2. Educational Activities, 1983, 33⅓ rpm, and 2000, compact disc. Liner notes.

Lee, Warren F., and Catherine T. Lee. *A Selective History of the Codornices-University Village, the City of Albany & Environs*. Albuquerque, NM: Belvidere Delaware Railroad Company Enterprises, 2000.

Richter, Bernadelle. Interview with the author. June 2016.

1956: Ella makes her first appearance on a Chicago-based children's television show called *Totem Club*. Soon she has her own musical segment on the show called "This Is Rhythm." Folk singer Odetta and bluesman Big Bill Broonzy are among her guests. From this point on, Ella considers herself a "full-time freelance musician."

1957: Ella releases *Call-and-Response Rhythmic Group Singing*. It is the first of her more than 60 albums for children.

1960: Alvin Ailey American Dance Theater, an African American dance company, premieres *Revelations*, which will become their signature piece. It features music written and arranged by Ella. In the 1960s, Ella meets Bernadelle Richter, who becomes Ella's manager and lifelong companion.

1964: To highlight how unsafe and unfair housing is for Black people in Chicago, Dr. Martin Luther King Jr. holds a rally at Chicago's Soldier Field. Many musicians perform, including Ella.

1968: Dr. King is assassinated in Memphis, Tennessee.

1974: Ella makes her first appearance on *Mister Rogers' Neighborhood*. Her last appearance will be in 1992.

2004: Ella receives a Grammy Lifetime Achievement Award.

2017: Ella releases her 62nd album: *Camp Songs with Ella Jenkins & Friends*.